Hi, I'm Darla!
My favorite things in the whole
world are coloring, gymnastics, and space.
When I grow up, I'm going to be an astronaut
and be the first person to walk on Mars.

Astronautica

Twinkie

Let's have fun coloring as we learn about our *Super Girl* mindset together!

I start each day with a

grateful

HEART

I am grateful FOR...

TODAY IS FULL OF POSSIBILITIES

I HAVE THE

POWER
TO
CHOOSE!

MY FRIENDS

MY FEELINGS

MY ATTITUDE

MY MANNERS

MY ACTIONS

MY WORDS

MY REACTIONS

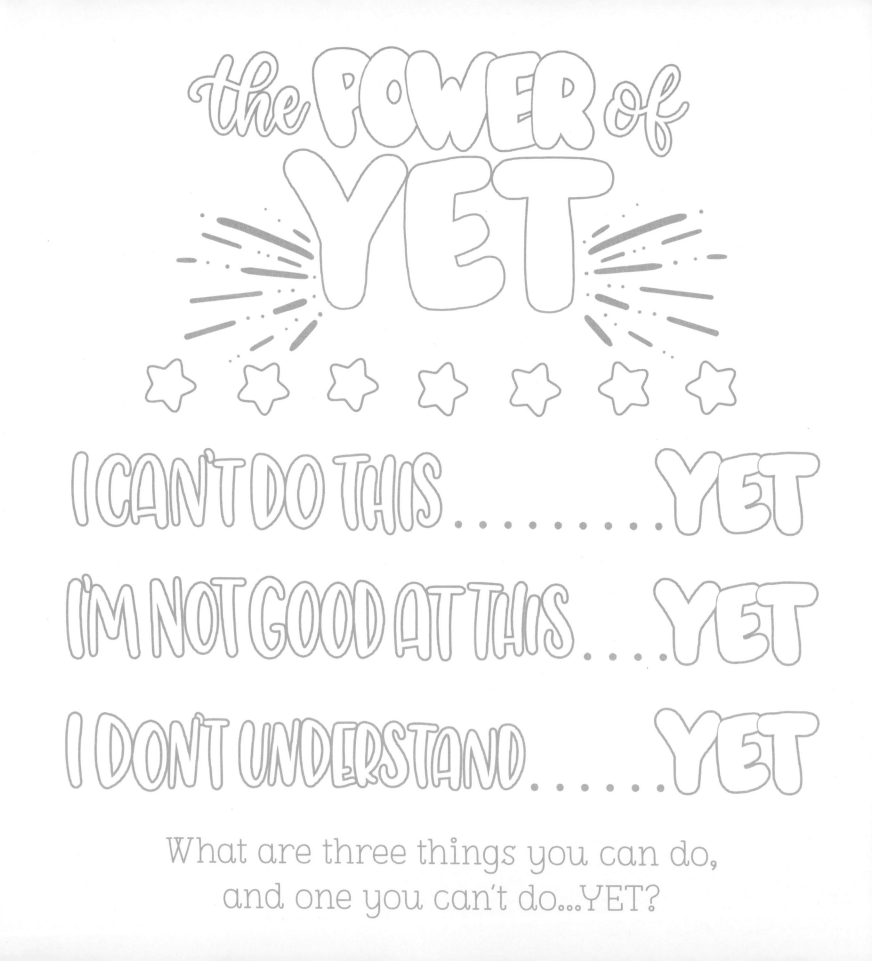

the POWER of YET

I CAN'T DO THIS . . . . YET

I'M NOT GOOD AT THIS . . . . . YET

I DON'T UNDERSTAND . . . . . . YET

What are three things you can do,
and one you can't do...YET?

MY BRAIN GETS STRONGER WHEN I TRY HARD

Anything can be
FUN
with the right
MINDSET

I make HEALTHY choices

What healthy foods do you like to eat?

I LOVE myself

WHEN I LOVE MYSELF, IT'S EASIER TO LOVE OTHERS

Isn't it funny that we can ONLY SEE our OUTSIDES, but it's what's INSIDE that truly MATTERS

What do you LOVE MOST about HOW YOU LOOK?

"My FRECKLES – they're like GLITTER on my FACE!"

What do you LOVE MOST about HOW YOU LOOK?

I AM

I AM
confident

I'm Darla

Anyone can be brave if they keep taking small steps in the right direction

and I CHOOSE
to be BRAVE

I WISH
I was
BIGGER

said Darla

Size doesn't matter when **YOU** can **CHANGE** the **WORLD**

answered Astronautica

I like to
FILL MY CUP
with....

HAPPINESS

LAUGHTER

FRIENDSHIP

PLAY

LOVE

KINDNESS

COURAGE

GRATITUDE

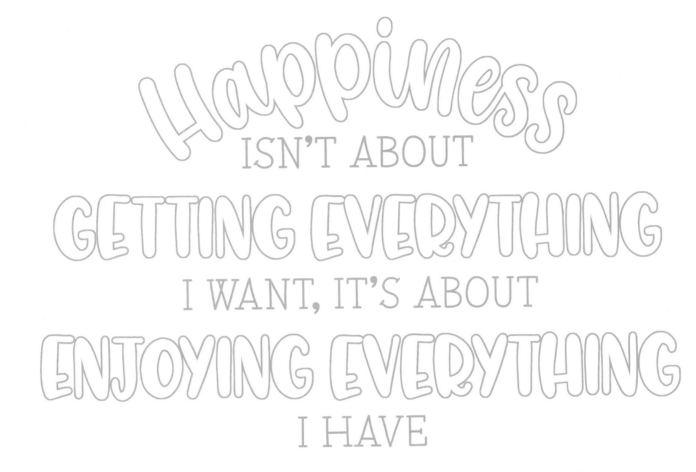

Happiness
ISN'T ABOUT
GETTING EVERYTHING
I WANT, IT'S ABOUT
ENJOYING EVERYTHING
I HAVE

WHAT MAKES YOU HAPPY?

MY FAMILY

ZOE

ASTRONAUTICA/TWINKIE

ICE CREAM/CUPCAKES

LEARNING ABOUT SPACE

Darla

I CAN MAKE THE WORLD A Better place

CAN MAKE A **BIG** DIFFERENCE

FRIENDS MAKE
ORDINARY MOMENTS
MAGICAL

Horses

I CHOOSE TO MOVE MY BODY IN A FUN WAY

What helps you feel better when you're sad?

MY IMAGINATION CAN TAKE ME ANYWHERE

Any Dream can Come True with a Good Plan and Hard Work

I DON'T HAVE TO BE *Perfect* TO BE AMAZING

Congratulations!

_____

name

HAS A **Super Girl** MINDSET!

She is grateful, kind, confident, and brave.

She uses her **Power to Choose** wisely

and always tries her best.

Keep up the great work!

MORE BOOKS FROM THE AUTHORS:

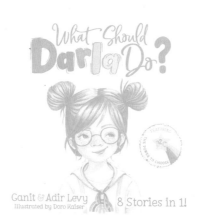

COMING SOON:

What Should Danny Do? On Vacation

What Should Darla Do? At the Carnival

To stay updated on new releases,
join us at www.whatshoulddarlado.com

What Should Darla Do? Super Girl Mindset Coloring Book / by Ganit & Adir Levy.

Summary: An empowering coloring book that teaches growth mindset, kindness, and confidence.
Levy, Ganit & Adir, authors
Kaiser, Doro, illustrator
Layne, Shannon, hand lettering
ISBN 9781733094627
Visit www.whatshoulddarlado.com
Printed in China
Reinforced binding
First Edition, November 2020
10 9 8 7 6 5 4 3 2 1